Rock Stars

MINERALS

Chris and Helen Pellant

Tick Tock Books

Copyright © *TickTock* Entertainment Ltd. 2008
This edition produced for Scholastic Inc. 2010
First published in Great Britain in 2008 by *TickTock* Entertainment Ltd.,
The Old Sawmill, 103 Goods Station Road, Tunbridge Wells, Kent TN1 2DP, U.K.

ticktock project editor: Julia Adams
ticktock project designer: Emma Randall
ticktock picture researcher: Lizzie Knowles
series consultant: Terry Jennings

We would like to thank Graham Rich, James Powell, and Joe Harris.

ISBN: 978-1-84696-695-8
Tracking number: 3375LPP1209

Printed in China
9 8 7 6 5 4 3 2 1

Picture credits (t=top; b=bottom; c=center; l=left; r=right; OFC=outside back cover;
OBC=outside back cover):
age fotostock/Superstock: 20tr. Jon Arnold Images Ltd./Alamy: 7. E. R. Degginger/Science Photo
Library: 22ft. ephotocorp/Alamy: 11b. Patrice Fury/Rex Features: 22t. GC Minerals/Alamy: 23cl.
Jennie Hart/Alamy: 15br. Herris.fr/SuperStock: 5t. David Martyn Hughes/Alamy: 3l, 21br. iStock:
OFC main, 4l, 5br, 6c, 10bcA, 14cr, 15bl, 15cr, 23tr, 23bl. David Lees/Corbis: 10bcC. *The Artist's Parents*,
1813 (panel), Wilkie, Sir David (1785–1841)/© National Gallery of Scotland, Edinburgh, Scotland/The
Bridgeman Art Library: 10bcB. Chris and Helen Pellant: 7tr, 10blC, 13tr, 13br, 14bl, 15tr, 16tl, 16cl, 16tr,
16cr, 16br, 17tl, 17bl, 18tl, 18br, 19cr, 19br, 20cl, 20cr, 20bl, 20br, 21tl, 21bl, 21tr, 23br, 24tl. Scientifica/Visuals
Unlimited/Alamy: 12l. Shutterstock: OFCt x 3, 1, 2, 3 A, B, C, D, E, F, G, H, J, K, 4tl, 4c, 4r, 5bl, 5bc, 6tl, 6b, 8tl,
8cl, 8–9, 9t, 9b, 10tl, 10cr, 12tl, 12cr, 12bl, 12br, 14tl, 14bc, 14br x 2, 15tl, 15cl, 15bl, 15br, 16bl, 17cl, 17tr,
17cr, 17br, 18tr, 18cr, 18bl, 19tl, 19tr, 19cl, 19bl, 20tl, 21cl, 21cr, 22b, 23tl, 23cr, OBC. Andrew Syred/Science
Photo Library: 8bl. Javier Trueba/Science Photo Library: 22c. Visual Arts Library (London)/Alamy:
11t. Charles D. Winters: 10blB

Every effort has been made to trace copyright holders, and we apologize in advance for any
omissions. We would be pleased to insert the appropriate acknowledgments in any
subsequent edition of this publication.

Contents

Words that appear in **bold** are explained in the glossary.

What Are Minerals?

Minerals are chemicals that occur naturally in the ground. There are many different types of minerals. They come in a lot of different shapes and colors.

Minerals are the basic parts from which rocks are made. All rocks are made of at least one mineral, but most contain two or more.

Some minerals are soft and powdery.

Sometimes, minerals can be very hard and shiny.

Minerals can form many different types of rocks.

It's a Fact!

There are more than 3,900 different minerals on Earth.

This form of the mineral gypsum is called a desert rose.

Minerals are very important for plants, animals, and humans. We need the mineral calcium for our bones. We get calcium from milk. The salt in food is a mineral, too.

When you look around, you will see that we use minerals to make things, too. There are minerals in toothpaste, paint, and even plastic.

How Do Minerals Form?

Minerals can form in many different places. Most form deep under the ground. Others form on Earth's surface.

Mineral ingredients

Minerals are solid chemicals. These chemicals are often found in liquids. When the liquids are either heated up or cooled down, the chemicals in them harden and join to form minerals.

Minerals occur naturally. They are inorganic, which means that they do not come from animals or plants.

Citrine is made of the chemicals silicon and oxygen.

Where minerals form

Most minerals form deep under Earth's surface. This is where Earth is very, very hot and there is a lot of pressure. It is so hot that rock becomes **molten**. The chemicals in the rock **dissolve**. When the molten rock cools down, it hardens again and forms new minerals and rocks.

*Sometimes, molten rock bursts through a **volcano** and cools down on Earth's surface.*

From mineral to rock

Rocks can form when minerals join together. When rocks form from hot molten rock, they are called **igneous rocks**.

Sometimes, the pressure under Earth's surface changes minerals. This means they form new rocks. These are **metamorphic rocks**.

This is diorite. It is an igneous rock. It is made of the minerals feldspar and hornblende.

Some minerals form on the surface of Earth. A lot of them form when water **evaporates**. This is a picture of the Dead Sea in Israel. When the water evaporates there, salt is left over.

Mineral Shapes

We can find out the type of a mineral by looking at its shape. **Crystals** give every mineral its own shape. Crystals are shapes that have smooth **faces** and straight edges.

Some crystals make up a shape that looks the same from all sides. These crystals are symmetric.

<< This mineral is called quartz. It has crystals that form in long six-sided columns.

<< This picture was taken through a microscope. It shows the crystals of table salt. This mineral forms in **cube**-shaped crystals.

Other mineral shapes

There are also minerals that are not symmetrical.
They are often part of mineral displays because of their unusual shapes.

This is a mineral called **>>**
gypsum. This type of gypsum
is called desert rose because
it looks like the petals of a rose.
It forms in deserts around
the world.

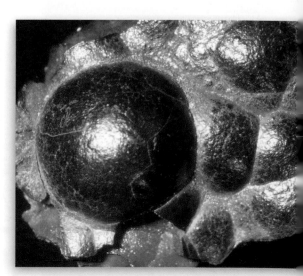

<< This is the mineral copper.
It can form in shapes that look
like plants. This type of shape
is called a dendritic shape.
Dendritic means "treelike."

This dark **>>**
red-brown mineral is
hematite. It often
forms in round
bubbly shapes.

Mineral Colors

Minerals come in many different colors. A mineral's color can help you identify which type of mineral it is. Colorful minerals have been used in many different ways for thousands of years.

Mineral paint

In the past, minerals were used to make paint. The paint was made by crushing the minerals. Then they were mixed with animal fat to make a paste.

realgar

In 1500 B.C., Egyptians started using the mineral realgar to create bright orange paint.

orpiment

The word *orpiment* comes from **Latin** and means "golden paint." It was used in many old paintings.

cinnabar

The mineral cinnabar was used to make bright red paint 900 to 600 years ago.

Today, we know that most of these minerals are poisonous.
This is why we don't use them for paint anymore.

a Roman woman using makeup

Mineral makeup

Many cultures have used powdered minerals as makeup. Women in ancient Rome used to whiten their skin with mineral powders that were made of **arsenic**. They did not know it was poisonous!

Mineral dye

For thousands of years, minerals such as lazurite have been used to make **dye**. Ancient cultures all over the world used powdered minerals to color their clothes.

It's a Fact!

Thousands of years ago, cavemen were the first people to use minerals for paintings.

Ancient Indian clothing was known for its brilliant colors. Many of the colors were made from minerals.

How Hard Are Minerals?

We use a scale with ten points to measure how hard a mineral is. You can use everyday things to test mineral hardness.

If you can scratch something with your fingernail, you know it is softer than 2.5 on the hardness scale.

It is easy to scratch some minerals, while others are much too hard. The hardness of a mineral is a good test when you are trying to figure out which mineral is which.

pocketknife blade: 5.5

Remember: always ask an adult to help you use a pocketknife. They are very sharp!

coins: 3.5

fingernails: 2.5

diamond: 10

corundum: 9

beryl: 8

quartz: 7

feldspar: 6

apatite: 5

fluorite: 4

calcite: 3

gypsum: 2

talc: 1

10 9 8 7 6 5 4 3 2 1

The small diamond in this picture is in a rock called kimberlite. There is a lot of this rock in South Africa. Many diamonds are found in **mines** there. Diamond is the hardest mineral.

It's a Fact!

You can also use another mineral to do a hardness test. A hard mineral will scratch a softer one.

Talc is the softest mineral. This specimen has many marks on it. This shows how easy it is to scratch talc.

How We Use Minerals

Minerals provide us with an amazing range of useful things. All of the metals we use, such as iron and copper, come from minerals.

Minerals in jewelry

Jewelry is made from minerals such as rubies, sapphires, and diamonds. These gemstones are all minerals. So are the metals silver and gold.

Hematite

This bubble-shaped mineral is made into iron. Under very high temperatures, iron can be turned into steel. Steel is used to build bridges and many other everyday items.

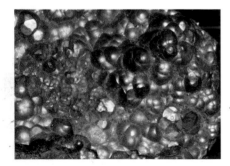

hematite

steel

steel bridge

saucepan

Chalcopyrite

This mineral is used to make the soft metal copper. People all over the world have made and used copper for thousands of years.

Gypsum

This soft mineral is dried and ground into powder. The gypsum powder is then used to make plaster.

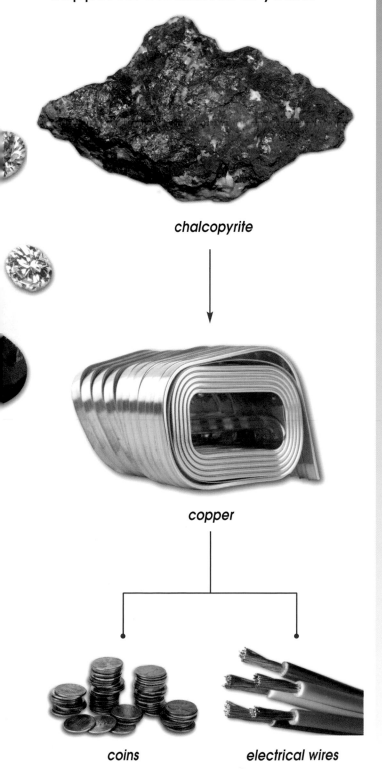

chalcopyrite

copper

coins   *electrical wires*

gypsum

gypsum powder

wall plaster   *plaster cast*

Mineral Collector

These minerals form in rocks:

Actinolite

COLOR:	green
PLACE FORMED:	in metamorphic rocks
HARDNESS:	5–6

Augite

COLORS:	black or dark green
PLACE FORMED:	in igneous rocks
HARDNESS:	5.5.–6

Garnet

COLORS:	red, green, yellow, black
PLACE FORMED:	in metamorphic rocks
HARDNESS:	6.5–7.5

Hornblende

COLORS:	black or dark green
PLACE FORMED:	in igneous rocks
HARDNESS:	5–6

Mica

COLORS:	silver, yellow, green, lilac, brown, black
PLACE FORMED:	in igneous and metamorphic rocks
HARDNESS:	2.5

Olivine

COLOR:	green
PLACE FORMED:	in igneous rocks
HARDNESS:	6.5–7

Feldspar

COLORS:	white, pink, gray
PLACE FORMED:	in igneous and metamorphic rocks
HARDNESS:	6

Kyanite

COLORS:	blue, green, yellow, black
PLACE FORMED:	in metamorphic rocks
HARDNESS:	5.5–7

Quartz

COLORS:	white, clear, pink, purple, yellow, brown, green, gray
PLACE FORMED:	in most rocks
HARDNESS:	7

Getting Started

In order to become a mineral collector, you need the following equipment:

- a sturdy backpack for your finds and equipment

- cloth or plastic bags to protect your specimens on the way home

- a rock hammer to break up loose rocks

- goggles to wear when hammering. Rock splinters may fly around and get in your eyes.

- a magnifying glass to see close-up details

- a notebook and a pen to write down details about the minerals you have collected

Mineral Collector

These minerals are found in mine heaps:

Arsenopyrite

COLOR: silver
PLACE FORMED: in mineral veins
HARDNESS: 5.5–6

Barite

COLORS: white, clear, yellow, gray
PLACE FORMED: in mineral veins
HARDNESS: 3–3.5

Cassiterite

COLORS: brown to black
PLACE FORMED: in mineral veins
HARDNESS: 6–7

Chalcopyrite

COLOR: shiny yellow
PLACE FORMED: in mineral veins
HARDNESS: 3.5–4

Galena

COLOR: gray
PLACE FORMED: in mineral veins
HARDNESS: 2.5

Siderite

COLORS: brown or yellow
PLACE FORMED: in mineral veins
HARDNESS: 4

Calcite

COLORS:	white, clear, gray, brown
PLACE FORMED:	in mineral veins; limestone
HARDNESS:	3

Fluorite

COLORS:	blue, purple, green, yellow, white
PLACE FORMED:	in mineral veins
HARDNESS:	4

Sphalerite

COLORS:	black or brown
PLACE FORMED:	in mineral veins
HARDNESS:	3.5–4

Finding Minerals

When mines are made, all of the soil and rocks that are dug out go on one big pile. This is called a mine heap. Mineral collectors can sometimes find many minerals in mine heaps.

Remember: if you visit the site of a mine, always go with an adult. Mines can be dangerous. Never enter an active mine.

Here are some other places where you can find minerals:

mineral veins

- **Mineral veins** running through rocks or across hillsides may be full of quartz and other minerals.

- Rocks are made of minerals. Look at the different-colored crystals in pebbles on the beach.

Mineral Collector

These minerals look great on display:

Agate

COLORS:	pink, red, blue
PLACE FORMED:	in some igneous rocks
HARDNESS:	7

Chrysocolla

COLORS:	green or blue
PLACE FORMED:	in copper layers
HARDNESS:	2–4

Gypsum

COLORS:	white, yellow, brown, green
PLACE FORMED:	in clay, dried-up salt lakes, and shallow seas
HARDNESS:	2

Pyrite

COLOR:	metallic pale golden yellow
PLACE FORMED:	in mineral veins and rocks, especially slate
HARDNESS:	6–6.5

Topaz

COLORS:	gray, yellow, green, brown, orange, purple
PLACE FORMED:	in granite
HARDNESS:	8

Tourmaline

COLORS:	green, pink, yellow, brown, black
PLACE FORMED:	in granite and metamorphic rocks
HARDNESS:	7–7.5

Dioptase

COLOR: dark green
PLACE FORMED: in mineral veins rich in copper
HARDNESS: 5

Rhodochrosite

COLORS: pink or red
PLACE FORMED: in mineral veins
HARDNESS: 3.5–4

Vanadinite

COLORS: red or orange
PLACE FORMED: in mineral veins
HARDNESS: 3

Your Display

When you have collected some mineral samples, you can display them.

Here are a few tips on how to display your mineral samples:

- Specimens should be very carefully cleaned with a soft paintbrush.

- Make cardboard trays for your specimens.

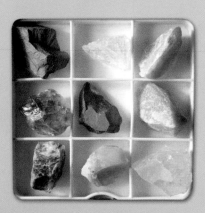

- Make labels for each mineral saying what it is and where you found it.

- Your display can be kept in a glass-fronted cupboard or on a shelf. Other minerals can be kept in drawers.

Record Breakers

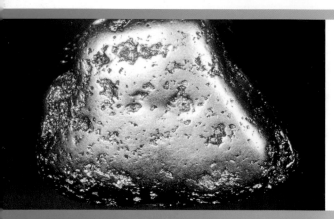

Most precious metal

Platinum is the most valuable metal.
It is worth around twice as much as gold.
It is used to make jewelry, watches, car
exhausts, and even in chemical factories.

*two of the big diamonds
cut from Cullinan*

Largest gem diamond

The Cullinan diamond is the biggest gem
diamond ever found. It was discovered in
South Africa and weighed 21.92 oz. (621.35g).
It was around the size of a grapefruit!
Cullinan was broken down into nine big
diamonds and 96 smaller diamonds.

Biggest crystals

The Cave of Crystals in Chihuahua,
Mexico, has the largest crystals in the
world. They are made of gypsum and
take millions of years to form.

Most common mineral
on Earth's surface

Naturally formed ice is a mineral, even
though water isn't. It is the most common
mineral on Earth's surface. It covers at least
ten percent of our planet.

Did You Know?

Diamonds are so hard that they cannot be scratched by anything. They are 40 times harder than talc.

The ancient Egyptians were one of the earliest cultures to make jewelry and other precious items from gold.

Gold is a very soft mineral. You can scratch it with a coin!

Fool's gold is a gold-colored mineral also known as pyrite. It looks like real gold, but it is much harder.

Some clocks use a very thin slice of quartz to keep time. The regular vibrations of the quartz help precisely measure time.

The mineral realgar forms in bright red crystals. People used to use it to color fireworks until they discovered that it was poisonous.

The Statue of Liberty in New York City is colored green. This is because it is coated with the mineral atacamite.

Minerals don't exist only in rocks. Your bones and teeth are made of inorganically formed minerals, too.

Sometimes, minerals form in rock cracks. These shapes are called mineral veins.

Glossary

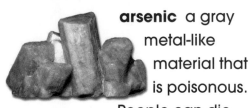

arsenic a gray metal-like material that is poisonous. People can die from arsenic poisoning.

chemical a substance that occurs naturally. Chemicals can be liquid, solid, or gaseous.

crystal a solid mineral form. It has straight edges and smooth faces.

cube a solid shape with six square sides, like a die

dissolve to become part of a liquid. For example, sugar dissolves in hot liquids.

dye a substance that can color clothes or hair

evaporate when something liquid turns into a gas. Water evaporates when it turns into water, vapor, or steam.

face the flat shiny surface of a crystal

igneous rock a type of rock formed from hot molten rock deep under the ground. When the molten rock bursts to Earth's surface, it can form igneous rock there, too.

Latin a language that used to be spoken by the ancient Romans

metamorphic rock a type of rock that has been changed from what it was at first. These changes are caused by heat or pressure deep under the ground.

mineral vein a mass of minerals that form in cracks in rocks or between rock layers

mine a very deep hole in Earth. People dig mines to find minerals and crystals that are deep under the ground.

molten extremely hot and liquid

volcano a hole in Earth's crust where molten rock bursts to the surface

Index